cyber attack

martin gitlin and
margaret j. goldstein

TWENTY-FIRST CENTURY BOOKS
MINNEAPOLIS

Twenty-First Century Books
A division of Lerner Publishing Group, Inc.
241 First Avenue North
Minneapolis, MN 55401 USA

Main body text set in Caecilia COM 55 Roman 9.5/14
Typeface provided by Linotype AG.

For reading levels and more information, look up this title at www.lernerbooks.com.

Library of Congress Cataloging-in-Publication Data

Gitlin, Martin.
    Cyber attack / by Martin Gitlin and Margaret J. Goldstein
        pages   cm
    Includes bibliographical references and index.
    ISBN: 978–1–4677–2512–5 (lib. bdg. : alk. paper)
    ISBN: 978–1–4677–6304–2 (EB pdf)
        1. Computer crimes—Juvenile literature. 2. Computer crimes—Prevention—Juvenile literature. 3. Computer security—Juvenile literature. I. Title.
    HV6773.G52 2015
    364.16'8—dc23   2014012242

Manufactured in the United States of America
1 – VI – 12/31/14

CONTENTS

The New "Most Wanted"

THE TEN MOST WANTED LIST, PUBLISHED BY THE US FEDERAL BUREAU OF INVESTIGATION (FBI), IS POPULATED BY THE USUAL SUSPECTS: kidnappers, murderers, armed robbers, rapists, and money launderers. But that's old school.

Since 2013 the FBI has been posting a Cyber's Most Wanted list, which enlists Americans to help in the hunt for the top online crooks. These are criminals for the twenty-first century, wanted for hijacking Internet traffic, cyber spying on businesses and governments, tracking computer users' keystrokes to steal passwords and financial information, breaking into online bank accounts, installing malicious software (malware) on computers, and much more.

As the FBI list demonstrates, cyber crime is serious business. According to the Internet security company Norton, cyber crimes cost consumers worldwide about $113 billion in 2013. McAfee, another Internet security firm, reports that cyber crimes cost businesses around the world almost $500 billion each year. Technology experts have developed security software to protect

The FBI's Cyber's Most Wanted list includes hackers and hacking rings that have committed cyber crimes against individuals, businesses, or organizations in the United States.

computers, but the attacks keep coming—and the "white hats," or computer security professionals, can barely keep ahead of the "black hats," or online criminals.

Attacks on computers have become more frequent—and more worrisome. Hackers have hit electrical power grids, oil and gas pipelines, and other critical national infrastructures. According to the US Department of Homeland Security, cyber attacks on critical US infrastructures numbered 198 in 2012, a 52 percent increase over the previous year.

Cyber criminals relentlessly attack corporate computers, trying to steal financial data, industrial blueprints, and business plans. The Internet is also awash in schemes to steal passwords from personal computers, which in turn can lead cyber thieves to credit card, Social Security, and bank account numbers. Some cyber criminals steal military secrets. Others disrupt the workings of governments and political organizations.

Many cyber crooks are lone individuals, working without associates. Others are allied into gangs—some of them well organized and even state funded. Many cyber criminals use botnets, or armies of robot computers, to inflict massive damage that could not be accomplished with individual computers alone. Who are these criminals and what motivates them? How can we stop them—and what might happen if we don't?

The New
"Most Wanted"

Chapter 1

Phreaks and Geeks

IN THE 1960S, LONG BEFORE PEOPLE ON EARTH WERE CONNECTED VIA THE INTERNET, PEOPLE WERE ALREADY CONNECTED BY TELEPHONE. The long-distance telephone network was extensive, but it was expensive to use. It cost a lot to call someone in another city, state, or nation. Telephone technology was also a mystery to most ordinary people, and in 1962, some inquisitive students at Harvard University set out to decipher how it worked. The students were technology geeks, interested in the circuits, relays, and switchboards that enabled people to talk over wires. They also wanted to make free long-distance phone calls. They called themselves phone phreaks.

The phone phreaks studied every document about telephone technology they could find. They learned that by playing or whistling certain tones into a telephone receiver at a frequency of 2600 hertz (Hz), they could trick the phone system into opening a free long-distance phone connection. In the mid-1960s, a phone phreak named John Draper earned the nickname Captain Crunch after discovering that he could do the telephone trick using a cheap plastic whistle from a box of Cap'n Crunch breakfast cereal. Other phreaks built devices called blue boxes, which duplicated the 2600-Hz tone and other tones used by phone companies.

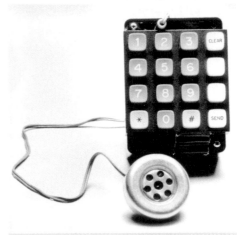

Beginning in the 1960s, phone phreaks built blue boxes such as this one to tap into phone systems and make free long-distance calls. Steve Wozniak and Steve Jobs, who became famous as the founders of Apple Inc., built this blue box in 1972.

As the phone phreaks learned more about telephone technology, they got together to share information. In 1973 one group started an underground magazine called *TAP*, for the Technological American Party. *TAP* and similar publications taught tricks of the phreaking trade, such as how to build blue boxes.

Tic Tech Toe

The late twentieth century saw the birth of a computer revolution. Business computers had been around since the early 1950s. But the old machines were expensive, enormous (just one could fill an entire room), slow, and limited in their computing abilities. By the mid-1970s, the computing landscape had drastically changed. Business computers had become smaller, faster, and more powerful. In 1975 Harvard dropout Bill Gates and his high school friend Paul Allen founded Microsoft, which produced software for personal computers. A year later, twenty-one-year-old Steve Jobs and twenty-six-year-old Steve Wozniak, along with business adviser Ron Wayne, founded

Phreaks and Geeks

Apple, which built both personal computers and the software to run them.

As the computer revolution ramped up, phone phreaks continued to make mischief inside telephone systems. Meanwhile, businesses and individuals started to connect multiple computers to one another using networks called bulletin board systems (BBSs), which operated via the phone lines. Since phone phreaks knew how to tap into phone lines, they quickly learned to tap into BBSs and the computers connected to them. From there, phreaking led to hacking. Some hackers even combined the two terms and called themselves phrackers.

The Internet gave hackers an even bigger stage on which to perform. The network had begun in 1969 as a US Defense Department project called the Advanced Research Projects Agency Network, or ARPANet. It initially linked military, government, and university computers. In the 1980s, as the Internet grew to include more and more users, hackers used it to infiltrate business and government computers. Individual hackers began to join forces. In 1983, for example, a hacking group in Milwaukee, Wisconsin, known as the 414s (named for the local area code) broke into the computers of sixty organizations. One of these was the Los Alamos National Laboratory in New Mexico, where scientists develop nuclear bombs. Other hacker groups infiltrated military installations, hospitals, and banks. To share techniques with one another, hackers published books and magazines and held conferences.

Infection!

In the twenty-first century, most people associate malicious software with criminals. But the first people to create malware did not have criminal motives—they simply wanted to learn more about computers. For instance, Fred Cohen was an engineering student at the University of Southern California in Los Angeles in 1983 when he created the first computer virus.

Famous Phreaks

In 1971 Steve Wozniak, then a student at the University of California–Berkeley, read a magazine article about phone phreaks. He was intrigued by the funny names they gave themselves to avoid detection. "I could tell that the characters being described were really tech people, much like me, people who liked to design things just to see what was possible, and for no other reason," Wozniak said many years later.

He described the phone phreaks to his friend Steve Jobs, who was still in high school. That afternoon they visited a technical library at nearby Stanford University and found an international phone manual that listed tone frequencies. With information from the manual, tone-generator kits from an electronics store, and a cassette tape recorder, the two young men built their own blue box. It didn't work. Back in class at Berkeley, Wozniak could not stop thinking about the blue box he and Jobs had created. So he designed another one, using computer chips for better tone accuracy and completing the project in early 1972. When he and Jobs tested the box, it worked the first time. They had become official phone phreaks.

The fun part was adopting character names. Jobs dubbed himself Oaf Tobar, while Wozniak became Berkeley Blue. The two young men went on to build more blue boxes and sold them to other phreaks. Soon they turned their attention to building and selling computers. The two founded the computer company Apple in 1976.

Viruses are programs that can alter the way a computer operates, without the permission or knowledge of the user, and they can replicate to infect multiple files. Cohen's virus infected only a few computers in a controlled university experiment.

In 1988 Robert Morris Jr., a graduate student in computer science at Cornell University in New York, created the first computer worm. Similar to viruses, worms are malicious programs that can replicate to infect multiple computers. Working on his own, without permission from the university, Morris created an experimental worm and injected it into the Internet to see how far it would travel. He released the worm from a computer at the Massachusetts Institute of Technology (MIT) rather than from a computer at Cornell to prevent others from learning the worm's source. Morris soon discovered that the worm was replicating at a much faster rate than he had expected. As it spread, it crashed thousands of computers at universities, military installations, and medical research facilities. Some repairs cost tens of thousands of dollars. Although Morris claimed that he had not meant any harm in releasing the worm, he was convicted of violating the Computer Fraud and Abuse Act of 1986. As punishment, he spent three years on probation, performed four hundred hours of community service, and paid a $10,000 fine.

> "I could tell that the characters being described were really tech people, much like me, people who liked to design things just to see what was possible."
>
> — Steve Wozniak, Apple cofounder, discussing early 1970s phone phreaks, 2013

Troublemakers

In the 1990s, the Internet exploded. Between 1993 and 1996, the number of registered Internet protocol (IP) addresses (each computer on the web has its own IP address) climbed from 1.3 million to 9.5 million. Along with this growth, hacking became more widespread—and more sinister. Hackers worked worldwide, with many high-profile attacks originating in Russia, China, the United Kingdom, and the United States. Some hackers unleashed viruses and worms simply because they could. Others were more practical. They broke into bank computers and transferred millions of dollars into their own accounts at different banks. In 1996 a computer programmer named Timothy Lloyd, who had been fired from a job at a New Jersey engineering firm, took revenge by planting a "software time bomb" on the firm's computers. The bomb deleted software critical to the operation of the company and caused more than $10 million in lost business.

Hackers quickly realized that they could do a lot more damage using multiple computers than they could with only one machine. In 2000 a fifteen-year-old Canadian named Michael Calce, using the online alias Mafiaboy, installed malware on about two hundred university computer networks. Through his ploy, he was able to take control of thousands of individual computers. With this botnet (a term that combines the words *robot* and *network*), he directed the machines to bombard the search engine Yahoo! with requests for data. The botnet overwhelmed Yahoo! with so much traffic that legitimate users couldn't get through to the site. Because of this distributed denial of service (DDoS) attack, Yahoo! went off-line for about three hours. Over the next week, Mafiaboy launched DDoS attacks against eBay, CNN, Amazon, and Dell. The attacks cost the companies an estimated $1.7 billion in lost business.

By the first decade of the twenty-first century, as hackers perfected their criminal techniques, the Internet had become

Hack Job

The term *hacking* in connection to computers originated with phone phreaks at the Massachusetts Institute of Technology in 1963. In that year, the MIT student newspaper wrote about hackers breaking into university computer and phone systems. At first, tech experts used *hacking* in a more positive sense. They defined a hacker as anyone skilled at working with computer programs, languages, and systems. They used the term *cracker* for someone who hacked into computers for criminal or mischievous purposes.

Kevin Mitnick is a famous black hat–turned–white hat. After serving five years in prison for criminal hacking, committed during the 1980s and the 1990s, Mitnick opened a computer security consulting firm. He uses his hacking expertise to help businesses protect themselves from cyber criminals.

In the twenty-first century, the term *hacker* is commonly used in connection with cyber criminals. Yet many computer experts still use the positive definition of hacker. Some people call themselves ethical hackers. These experts try to penetrate computer networks to determine their security vulnerabilities. Businesses, governments, and other organizations hire them to locate the vulnerabilities and to remedy them, so that unethical hackers can't break into the systems.

Sometimes unethical hackers change their ways. They give up criminal hacking and take honest jobs as computer security experts. Kevin Mitnick is a famous example. After serving five years in prison in the late 1990s for criminal hacking, Mitnick went on to found Mitnick Security Consulting, a highly regarded computer security firm. He has also written several books about criminal hacking, including about his own experiences.

completely integrated into modern life. Paying bills, buying airplane tickets, sharing photos and videos with friends, searching for a job or a pet, and watching movies and TV—all of it could be done online.

In the second decade of the twenty-first century, especially in the industrialized world, most people use computers and the Internet at their jobs. Around the world, almost every government office, business, and university is computerized and connected to the web. But the billions of computer users on Earth are also potential victims of cyber crime. The Internet has become a cyber criminal playground.

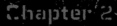

Chapter 2.

User
Beware

ONE DAY YOU CHECK YOUR E-MAIL AND
FIND A MESSAGE FROM A MUSIC WEBSITE
YOU VISIT OFTEN. The message contains an
"Important Notice." It says that the site has
detected unusual activity on your account and
has temporarily suspended it. You are directed to click on a
link to reactivate your account. At first you're tempted to click,
eager to get back on the site to listen to your favorite music. But
as a savvy Internet user, you're suspicious. The company logo
in the message looks just like the real thing. But the rest of the
message doesn't seem quite right. You notice a typo in the text,
and the domain name in the link you're supposed to click on
doesn't match the domain name at the top of the e-mail. You
do a Google search and find a host of articles about the very
e-mail you have just received. You were right—it's a phishing

e-mail, designed to get you to click on the link and to reveal your username and password to a criminal.

Phishing scams are so named because criminals fish for victims in the vast ocean of the Internet. These scams might take the form of a bogus e-mail or text message, a pop-up ad, or a web page designed to look like the real thing. Because users normally trust the business that appears to have created the message, they often click on the link provided. Sometimes, just clicking the link might lead to the installation of malware on a computer. And if a user goes on to type in a username, a password, or other personal information as directed, things can go from bad to worse. If an account is linked to a credit card, a Social Security number, or a bank account, the user has just given that information to a criminal.

Who falls for these scams? Millions of people do. That's how hackers make their money. According to Symantec's Security Technology and Response unit, 156 million phishing e-mails go online every day. Of those 156 million e-mails, about 16 million (roughly 10 percent) make it past spam filters installed by Internet service providers, businesses, and personal computer users. When those 16 million e-mails arrive in people's in-boxes, users open about half of them—roughly 8 million e-mails. At that point, most people recognize the scam and delete the e-mail. But about 10 percent of those who receive phishing e-mails (800,000 per day) click on links in the e-mails. And 10 percent of those who click on the links (80,000) share personal information with hackers.

Names and Numbers

What happens when someone steals personal information online? Dave Crouse of Bowie, Maryland, found out when hackers remotely installed keystroke malware on his computer. Unknown to Crouse, the malware sat on his machine, waiting for him to log into his online bank account. When he did, the software recorded

Keystroke malware sits on victims' computers, recording personal information such as passwords and bank account numbers.

his keystrokes—learning his username, password, bank account number, and answers to security questions tailored just for him. With this information, the hackers were able to make thousands of dollars in purchases using his debit card number.

When Crouse discovered the fraud, he closed his bank account and opened one at a different bank. But because the malware was still lurking on his computer, hackers hit the new account too. With Crouse's financial data in hand, the hackers opened credit card accounts in his name. In less than six months, hackers had purchased $900,000 in goods and services using his identity. The bills for these purchases arrived at his home.

Crouse contacted the banks and companies that believed he owed them money. He spent hundreds of hours trying to prove that he had been a victim of fraud and was not liable for the charges. Meanwhile, he fell behind in paying his legitimate bills, and his credit score—the rating that banks and other businesses use to assess a person's ability to pay back loans—plummeted. It took Crouse several years to resecure his identity and to get his finances back in order.

Pay Up—or Else

Shirley Vannatta of Columbus, Ohio, encountered another type of cyber crime. One spring day, Vannatta turned on a friend's computer to check her e-mail, but the machine didn't start up normally. Instead, Vannatta saw a blank white screen for thirty seconds and then a message claiming to be from the FBI. The message stated that the computer owned by Vannatta's friend had visited illegal pornographic websites and had been used to promote terrorism. As a result of this alleged activity, the message said, the FBI had locked the computer to prevent further illegal activity.

The computer had been locked, but not by the FBI. Instead, cyber criminals had infected the machine with ransomware, a type of malware that locks all computer files and creates phony warning messages. The warning told Vannatta that to unlock the computer, she would have to pay a $300 fine using a prepaid debit card, the type available at many superstores and drugstores. To pay the fine, she would have to type the personal identification number (PIN) from the debit card into the warning screen.

Vannatta and her friend quickly realized that they had been scammed. They didn't pay the fine, but they did have to pay $200 to a technician to remove the malware from the computer.

Taking the Bait

Vannatta and her friend didn't fall for the ransomware scam, but many people do. According to computer security experts, ransomware has been used to infect hundreds of thousands of personal and business computers. And criminals are raking in millions of dollars every year through the scam. One ransomware gang hauled in more than $400,000 in a single day. The scam started in 2009 in eastern Europe and was first used by Russian hackers. It has since spread across Europe and the United States. The hackers send messages claiming to be from different law enforcement agencies, such as the FBI, the US Department of Justice (DoJ), or similar agencies in Europe.

Researchers say that between 3 and 5 percent of victims take the bait and pay the ransom—even though doing so does not actually unlock their files. In addition to locking up computer files, ransomware also scours victims' machines to grab passwords, credit card numbers, and other personal data that can be used for monetary gain. So even people who don't fall for the ransom scam can be victimized through other avenues.

User
Beware

Creepy

Cassidy Wolf was no ordinary teenager. The young Californian was a beauty pageant champion and was preparing to compete in the Miss Teen USA pageant in the Bahamas. A few months before the pageant, the social networking site Facebook alerted her that someone from a different state had attempted to log in to her Facebook account. Soon after receiving that e-mail, Wolf received a much more disturbing e-mail, from someone claiming to have hacked into the camera on the computer in her bedroom. The hacker claimed to have taken nude photos of Wolf, doing what a person does "in the privacy of their own room," she later told reporters. The hacker wrote that the photos would not be made public if Wolf provided more explicit nude images of herself.

A hacker used Blackshades malware to take remote control of teen pageant winner Cassidy Wolf's computer. Using the computer's built-in camera, he took pictures of Wolf in her bedroom.

Wolf contacted the authorities, who launched an investigation and eventually arrested a nineteen-year-old college computer science major named Jared James Abrahams. Abrahams was charged with victimizing Wolf as well as up to 150 other young women. His criminal strategy involved using a program called Blackshades to gain remote control of women's computers and to then photograph them without their knowledge.

Blackshades has been nicknamed creepware since it's used by creepy people. With Blackshades, a hacker can do more than remotely operate a computer's camera. Hackers can also listen to private conversations using a computer's built-in microphone, track online activity, and record keystrokes to gain passwords. Security experts say that Blackshades has infected more than a half million computers around the world. Two young hackers developed the program in 2010. The men—a Swede and an American—were arrested in 2012 and 2013, respectively, after selling copies of their program for between $40 and $100 each and taking in more than $350,000 in sales. One Dutch teenager used his copy of Blackshades to take secret pictures of women and girls on about two thousand computers.

You Are Being Watched

Criminal hackers aren't the only ones watching computer users online. Google keeps track of each individual's searches; Facebook and Twitter keep track of each user's posts and preferences; and other websites keep track of each visitor's purchases, interests, and other personal information. A wide range of companies buy this data and analyze it to learn about people's likes and dislikes, health concerns, shopping habits, political affiliations, and other traits and interests. The companies then sell the information to government agencies, insurance companies, private investigators, debt collectors, banks, marketers, and other groups that want to know more about political, financial, shopping, and social trends, as well as the activities of individual computer users.

This tracking and data collection is not illegal. When a user signs up for a site such as Facebook, he or she must click on a terms-of-usage agreement, allowing the site to track and gather personal usage data. In addition, most business websites automatically install files called cookies on visitors' computers. These files track users' browsing and purchasing activity. Web browsers such as Firefox allow people to delete cookies, but many users prefer to leave them installed. Without cookies, people have to reenter usernames, passwords, and other log-in information every time they visit a website.

What about the government? Is it illegal for the government to spy on people online? That question moved front and center in June 2013 when Edward Snowden, a former computer systems administrator, began to leak damaging revelations. He provided journalists with tens of thousands of documents showing that the National Security Agency (NSA), a US government intelligence organization for which he had done work, was spying on people all over the world, many of them high-ranking officials of foreign nations. Snowden was deeply disturbed by what he knew about the NSA. He felt strongly that the agency was violating US citizens' right to privacy, as protected by the Fourth Amendment to the US Constitution.

Snowden's revelations showed that the NSA, sometimes with the cooperation of telecommunications companies, has

In the summer of 2013, Edward Snowden, a former contractor with the National Security Agency, told the world about extensive NSA cyber spying on US citizens, foreign governments, and foreign leaders.

From *1984* to 2013

The revelations about NSA surveillance of the private phone, e-mail, and online activities of citizens around the world resulted in a revival of interest in a legendary book, the science-fiction classic *1984*. Written by British author George Orwell in 1949, the novel depicts a futuristic totalitarian state, with an unchecked government snooping into the private lives of its citizens. In writing the novel, Orwell was influenced by the repressive tactics of the government of the former Soviet Union (a union of fifteen republics that included Russia).

Soon after Edward Snowden's initial revelations about the NSA, sales of *1984* on Amazon.com rose 166 percent within one twenty-four-hour period. The book landed on the website's "Movers and Shakers" list of hot titles. In a televised interview in December 2013, Snowden commented that the NSA spying he had brought into the spotlight was actually far worse than anything depicted in Orwell's book. He said, "The types of collection in the book—microphones and video cameras, TVs that watch us—are nothing compared to what we have available today. We have sensors in our pockets [smartphones] that track us everywhere we go. Think about what this means for the privacy of the average person."

extensively monitored the e-mails, social media activity, browsing history, and Google searches of average citizens—all without court authorization. The NSA has mined the servers of Facebook, YouTube, Skype, Google, and Apple to collect e-mails, photos, video chats, and other data involving US citizens and non-US citizens. The agency has also monitored the phone calls of millions of people around the world. It has also unlocked encryption programs designed to protect the privacy of personal e-mails, banking records, and medical records.

US government officials argue that the NSA data collection program is legal and is designed to root out terrorists who might be operating within or planning to attack the United States. Officials also say that Snowden's revelations might help terrorists figure out how to best evade NSA surveillance operations, severely damaging US efforts in the war on terror.

The Snowden Effect

Edward Snowden's revelations of NSA spying created a national and international backlash. In the United States, a federal court judge ruled in late 2013 that the NSA's phone surveillance program was unconstitutional. In spring 2014, the US House of Representatives passed a bill that would limit the bulk collection of US phone data. But until all the legal proceedings are finalized, the phone surveillance program remains in operation.

Meanwhile, foreign governments have denounced the NSA for spying on their citizens and leaders. Some non-US firms have canceled contracts with Cisco Systems, AT&T, and other businesses thought to have cooperated with the NSA in its data collection efforts. Some foreign organizations have moved their data from US cloud-storage servers to servers in Europe, where privacy laws are stronger. And around the world, big tech companies have added extra layers of encryption to protect their customers' data.

Some say that these measures might make it more difficult for the NSA to collect data but that ultimately the agency will succeed in its spying efforts. Said Fred Cate, a law professor at Indiana University, "It doesn't make a difference what you do with your data—the NSA is going to break into it."

> "We have sensors in our pockets [smartphones] that track us everywhere we go. Think about what this means for the privacy of the average person."
>
> — *Edward Snowden, former National Security Agency contractor and whistle-blower, 2013*

But Edward Snowden and others feel that privacy is a foundational principle of any democracy. Spying on citizenry, they believe, should never be tolerated in a free society. Snowden faces charges of espionage and other crimes in the United States and is currently living in exile in Russia. The US government views him as a fugitive from justice, but many others see him as a hero. Two newspapers, the *Guardian* of the United Kingdom and the US *Washington Post,* won the 2014 Pulitzer Prize for Public Service for publishing his revelations, and Snowden himself has won honors from journalism, privacy, and civil liberties organizations.

Chapter 3

No Business as Usual

WILLIE SUTTON, A US BANK ROBBER, STOLE MORE THAN $2 MILLION FROM BANKS DURING HIS CRIMINAL CAREER IN THE MID-TWENTIETH CENTURY. When Sutton was asked why he robbed banks, he allegedly replied, "Because that's where the money is." Were twenty-first-century cyber criminals to provide their reasons for attacking banks and other big companies, they'd probably say the same thing.

Some cyber criminals go right for the cash. In one recent audacious heist, hackers stole $45 million from automated teller machines (ATMs) around the world. The operation began when hackers infiltrated the computers of an Indian credit-card-processing company. Once inside the system, the hackers raised withdrawal limits on five prepaid debit card accounts issued by Rakbank in the United Arab Emirates. The hackers gave the account numbers to crews in twenty countries, including the

United States. The crews encoded the numbers on the magnetic strips of blank bank cards and made forty-five hundred ATM transactions on December 21, 2012, stealing $5 million in cash on that day alone. The gang struck again two months later, in February 2013, this time raising withdrawal limits on twelve prepaid card accounts with the Bank Muscat in Oman. With the new account numbers, starting at 3 p.m. on February 19, 2013, crews in more than twenty-five countries made thirty-six thousand withdrawals from ATMs over ten hours. The total take in that time frame was $40 million.

Authorities in more than a dozen countries investigated the heists. Some of the crooks were brazen and posed with pictures of themselves with fat stacks of cash—making them easier to track down. Police picked up two Dutch suspects in Germany in late February 2013. US police arrested seven

Cyber thieves pose with money looted from ATMs in the New York area after heists in late 2012 and early 2013. Using stolen debit card numbers embedded on blank bank cards, these men and others took about $45 million in cash from ATMs around the world.

New York–based suspects in May and another six in November. Eight additional suspects—six Romanian citizens and two Moroccans—were arrested in Spain in December. According to news reports, one of those arrested was the mastermind of the heist, while the others were members of the cashing crews who took out money at ATMs. Other suspects remain at large.

Bilked in Brazil

In Brazil, people and businesses commonly pay bills, invoices, rent, mortgages, school tuition, and other fees using an electronic transfer system called Boleto Bancário. Payers initiate the transactions, nicknamed boletos, at banks or via their own computers. The system transfers money from one bank account to another. More than six billion boleto payments were made in Brazil in 2013 alone. The system is a convenient alternative to sending checks through the mail.

Boleto Bancário is not hacker-proof, however. In 2012 security researchers discovered that cyber criminals had been using malware to intercept boleto payments and divert them into their own bank accounts. In 2014 researchers revealed that over two years, a single criminal operation—called the bolware gang or bolware ring by authorities—had intercepted nearly a half million boletos from almost two hundred thousand personal computers. No one is sure how much of that money ended up in the gang's bank accounts, but it could total as much as $3.75 billion in US dollars.

How can boleto users protect themselves? Banks have directed them to install security plug-ins on their computers before using the system, but the bolware gang's malware disables the plug-ins. It also steals usernames and passwords from victims' PCs. Security experts also advise users to make their transactions using mobile devices instead of PCs, since the boleto malware doesn't work on smartphones—at least not yet. As of summer 2014, the authorities had not apprehended any bolware gang suspects.

Charge It

Cyber criminals in eastern Europe have taken a different approach to cashing in. Starting in 2005 and ending with their arrest in 2012, four Russian and one Ukrainian hacker tapped into the computers of credit card processors and other businesses. They stole 160 million credit card numbers, as well as PINs, selling the data to resellers for ten to fifty dollars per credit card number. The resellers encoded the numbers onto blank plastic cards to create fake credit and debit cards, which were then sold on the street and on underground credit card websites. People who bought the fake cards and PINs used them to withdraw cash at ATMs and to charge purchases. Yet the bills went to people whose card numbers had been stolen. The cost to the companies that had been hacked, which had to reimburse customers for fraudulent charges on their accounts, was $300 million.

Another devastating attack occurred between November 27 and December 15, 2013, when eastern European hackers hit the US department store giant Target during the busy Christmas shopping season. The hackers had discovered that Target's computer systems were vulnerable. Hackers easily installed malware on the in-store systems that allow customers to make payments by swiping credit and debit cards. The malware copied data encoded on the cards, moved it to Target's own servers, and from there sent it to a server in Russia. The criminals devised a clever way to cover their tracks, using a type of malware known as a memory scraper to delete most of the evidence of their crime.

In just over two weeks, the hackers siphoned up to 40 million credit and debit card numbers, along with PINs and card verification value numbers, used for extra security in credit card purchases. The hackers stole nonfinancial information, such as

In 2013 hackers installed malware on computer systems at Target, a big US department store chain. When customers swiped their debit or credit cards at the checkout counter, malware copied their card numbers, PINs, and other financial information.

27

names, addresses, e-mail addresses, and phone numbers, for up to 70 million other Target customers.

By the time the theft was discovered in mid-December, fake credit cards made with the stolen data had already shown up on the black market. Customers were also starting to see fraudulent charges on their credit card statements.

Target advised customers to search their credit and debit card statements for unauthorized charges, to order replacement cards, and to change their passwords and PINs. Although credit card issuers covered most of the losses suffered by cardholders—and Target then reimbursed the credit card issuers—customers still had to go through red tape to cancel their cards and to contest fraudulent charges.

Target customers were furious at the company for not securing its data. A woman named Melissa Milligan Gunter railed on the company's Facebook page, "Dear Target, thanks for making me (and so many others) have to go through and change everything [account information] that I use my debit and credit cards for because you can't keep your customer's information private."

Fearful of further security breaches, customers took their business elsewhere after the attack was revealed. Target's profits for the holiday shopping period fell 46 percent from the same period the year before. Customers and banks filed more than ninety lawsuits against Target for its negligence in securing customer data. The company had to pay fines to credit-card-industry regulators. To shore up customer loyalty, the company offered free credit monitoring for tens of millions of customers. The security breach cost Target hundreds of millions of dollars. One analyst put the cost to the company at $420 million.

Meanwhile, investigators followed the hackers' trail to Russia when they discovered that the virus used to breach Target's firewall had been nicknamed Kaptoxa, slang for "potato" in Russian. They also found the name Rescator in the code used by the hackers. That was the name of a black market website used to sell fake credit cards and also the alias of the Ukrainian hacker who ran it. As of mid-2014, thousands of stolen credit card numbers from the Target heist were still being sold on the black market and the authorities hadn't apprehended Rescator or anyone else thought to be involved in the crime.

Endless Assaults

The Target cyber attack made the news because of its massive size. In addition, the company believed that immediately going public about the hack would help preserve its reputation as a business that cares about its customers. The shipping company UPS, the supermarket chain Supervalu, and the hardware giant Home Depot also acknowledged that in 2014 hackers had hit their cash register systems and stolen customer data, but these companies are the exception. Most businesses that are hit by cyber attacks keep them secret because they don't want to shake the confidence of their customers and shareholders. They want to preserve the illusion that they are financially strong and impenetrable to cyber crimes. Nothing could be further from the truth.

In 2013 the broadband and telecommunications giant Verizon surveyed fifty businesses, government offices, and other organizations in ninety-five countries to assess the extent of attacks on their computer systems. According to the resulting 2014 *Verizon Data Breach Investigations Report,* the fifty groups suffered almost 63,500 "security incidents"—or attempted attacks—in 2013. Of these attempted attacks, 1,367 were successful. The crimes ranged from DDoS attacks to theft of financial data and industrial secrets. Multiplying these numbers by hundreds of thousands, to account for all the organizations in operation about the world, gives a sense of the broad scope of cyber crime the world over.

Attacks on businesses have become increasingly clever. In one case, hackers couldn't infiltrate the well-secured computers

The Darknet

Most legitimate business have an online presence, and many illegal businesses do as well. If a person wants to buy drugs, pornography, guns, a fake passport, or a fake credit card or wants to hire a hit man or a computer hacker, many web-based businesses will make the deal. This cyber underworld is called the darknet.

A darknet website called Silk Road made headlines in October 2013 when the FBI arrested its US operator, Ross Ulbricht, and shut down the site. Silk Road was a sort of underground Craigslist, where those who wanted to buy or sell illegal goods or services could connect. The site used secret servers in various countries to mask its activities and conducted business using Bitcoin, a virtual currency. Purchases were hidden behind a series of dummy transactions, to disguise the link between buyers and sellers. Silk Road took a cut of the money on each transaction.

The FBI uncovered Silk Road's secret servers in 2012 and set up a sting operation to catch Ulbricht. An FBI agent went undercover, posing on the site as a drug dealer with cocaine for sale. A Silk Road employee bought the drugs for $27,000 in Bitcoin. That sale led to the arrest of the employee as well as Ulbricht, along with a number of other buyers and sellers associated with the website. After the arrests, the FBI shut down the site, but within a few months, it was back in business, with new operators in charge and enhanced security to evade law enforcement. All the same, in a classic case of bad guy against bad guy, hackers stole $2.7 million in Bitcoin from Silk Road in February 2014.

of a big oil company, but they knew that a local Chinese restaurant was popular with its workers. The hackers' solution? They slipped malware into the restaurant's online menu.

As oil company employees perused the menu at lunch, they unknowingly downloaded the malicious code, which went on to infect the entire company network. Other hackers have inserted malware into printers, air conditioners, videoconferencing equipment, and other devices connected to business networks. Hackers have even entered via digital vending machines. In June 2014, a group of Chinese hackers smuggled malware into the networks of US and overseas military contractors and research companies using e-mailed invitations to golf outings.

Infected USB drives, also called flash drives and thumb drives, are often used to insert malware into computers. In 2010 a group of Chinese spies posed as businessmen at a British trade fair. They handed out free USB drives and other souvenirs to conference-goers who visited their booth. The drives appeared to be brand new and unused, but they had been preloaded with malware. When people who picked up the souvenir drives used them at work, they inadvertently unleashed spyware onto their company computers.

At many offices, workers routinely use flash drives to move data from one computer to another. But if USB drives are secretly loaded with malware, they can give cyber spies and cyber thieves access to computer networks.

Since computer systems, large and small, are endlessly under attack by cyber criminals, many insurance companies have begun to offer cyber attack insurance to cover business losses from online attacks. In 2013 US companies spent about $1.3 billion on cyber theft insurance.

Bad News Bots

Commanders rallied their troops to "FIRE FIRE FIRE FIRE." One leader urged, "If you are firing manually, keep firing....Don't switch targets, together we are strong!"

But the attack—launched by the international hacker group Anonymous against the online money transfer company PayPal— was not working. Anonymous wanted to take down PayPal's website with a DDoS attack in retaliation for PayPal refusing to do business with the whistle-blower website WikiLeaks. But the hacker group needed more firepower, so it brought in tens of thousands of bots. With this army of remotely controlled computers, Anonymous bombarded PayPal's servers with so much data that legitimate site users couldn't get through to do business. The site crashed and stayed down for an hour.

This was just the first assault in a campaign that Anonymous had dubbed Operation Payback. After PayPal, the hackers hit MasterCard, one of the world's biggest credit card companies, bringing its website down for twelve hours and crippling its ability to process customer transactions. On the same day, Anonymous took down the website of Visa, another credit card company, for twelve hours.

Anonymous's takedowns of the corporate websites caused only minor financial damage to businesses that bring in billions of dollars per year in revenues, but the attacks were still significant. They showed the power of botnets. These networks of computer robots are effective because they give those at the controls tremendous computing power. And with so many computers involved in an attack, law enforcement agencies have a difficult time tracking the attacks to the criminals in charge. It's like looking for a needle in a haystack.

To amass botnets, cyber criminals use malware to infect a network of computers, turning them into cyber zombies that will obey a botmaster's commands. Most computers are turned into bots without the knowledge of their owners. Once a computer becomes part of a botnet, the owner might notice that it operates slowly, displays strange messages, or crashes.

In addition to DDoS attacks, cyber criminals use botnets to send out millions of spam e-mails, phishing e-mails, and viruses. Botnets can also charge purchases using stolen credit card numbers on thousands of websites.

Often botnets are used to trick advertisers into thinking that a website has more visitors than it really does. Website operators want a lot of hits, because the more visitors a site has, the more money it can charge companies to advertise there. To boost their numbers, some websites make deals with botnet operators to flood their sites with hundreds of thousands of fake clicks. They can then boast to advertisers about the popularity of their websites and raise advertising rates accordingly. Bots can also flood Facebook, Twitter, and similar social-networking sites with "likes" and retweets to build up or knock down the popularity of a product, a celebrity, or a political candidate.

Security experts have devised several ways to distinguish between bots and real people visiting websites. One familiar device is the CAPTCHA, which stands for completely automated public Turing test to tell computers and humans apart. CAPTCHA was originally designed to prevent bots from taking part in online polls, elections, message boards, product reviews, and other activities where they might create misinformation. This online test requires a person submitting information to a website to retype a set of letters and numbers shown in distorted form. This task is fairly easy for humans but not so easy for computers. However, some computer programs can cheat the test, so its usefulness is limited. In addition, botmasters go to great lengths to make bots act like real people. Some bots interact with others online using ordinary human names, go online in the daytime and sign off at night, and even share photos and common observations such as LOL.

Chapter 4

Cool War with China

IN 2008 AN EMPLOYEE OF ALCOA INC. WAS BUSY AT WORK, PREPARING FOR A SHAREHOLDERS' MEETING. Among the employee's many e-mails was one from a familiar name—a member of the company's board of directors—with an attachment labeled agenda.zip. It looked like a normal business communication, so the employee clicked on the attachment. However, the e-mail was not from a board member, and it didn't contain the meeting agenda. Instead, it came from hackers affiliated with People's Liberation Army (PLA) Unit 61398, a Chinese military command. When the Alcoa employee opened the e-mail attachment, malware infected Alcoa's computer network and started gathering confidential financial and technical information.

Based in Pittsburgh, Pennsylvania, Alcoa is a global leader in lightweight metals mining, engineering, and manufacturing. Its products—made of aluminum, titanium, and nickel—are used in the manufacture of spacecraft, aircraft, military vehicles, automobiles, electronics, oil- and gas-drilling equipment, building materials, and manufacturing equipment. The malware secretly installed on Alcoa's computers in 2008 delivered the company's confidential business plans and manufacturing secrets directly to Unit 61398.

Alcoa wasn't the only target of the Chinese hacker attack that year. The same group used malware to steal secrets from US Steel, United Steelworkers, Westinghouse, Allegheny Technologies, and SolarWorld—all in Pennsylvania. And the attacks were just the tip of the iceberg. Security experts have identified more than twenty Chinese hacking crews affiliated with Unit 61398. In addition, experts have uncovered more than a dozen other hacking units connected to the Chinese army and navy and have traced the groups to hundreds of attacks on US businesses.

Security experts think Chinese hackers might have gathered technical data about the F-35 Joint Strike Fighter, a US military jet. If the Chinese military does have such information, China could build a similar plane without investing in expensive research. China might even use the data to figure out how to disable F-35s in the event of war with the United States.

Spy versus Spy

Since the first decade of the twenty-first century, Chinese hacking crews have stolen technology blueprints, pricing documents, negotiation strategies, and other information from hundreds of US companies. Chinese hackers have stolen source code from Google and data concerning the quantity, value, and location of oil fields from Marathon Oil, Exxon Mobil, and ConocoPhillips. Other US corporate victims of Chinese hackers have included Morgan Stanley, Symantec, Adobe, Dow Chemical, and Yahoo!

When Coca-Cola was in negotiations to purchase a big Chinese beverage company in 2009, it had no idea that a Chinese hacking unit was stealing sensitive internal documents about its finances throughout the entire course of the negotiations. An FBI cyber security unit that was monitoring Chinese hackers discovered the Coca-Cola hack and told Coca-Cola about the breach. After that, the business deal fell apart. Like many companies that are victims of hacking, Coca-Cola kept the incident secret for several years and has never revealed specifics about the company information that was stolen.

In 2012 Bloomberg News—an international news agency headquartered in New York—published an article about how relatives of China's vice president had grown rich from corrupt business dealings. Shortly afterward, Bloomberg was hit by hackers. In late 2012 and early 2013, hackers hit the *New York Times* after it printed a similar article about relatives of China's prime minister. Hackers infiltrated the e-mail accounts and personal computers of the news organizations' reporters and their business contacts. They appeared to be looking for the reporters' sources—those who had provided the damaging information about China's leaders—to intimidate them and to prevent additional articles on the subject from being printed.

When asked about suspicions that the *Times* hack had originated with Chinese military units, China's Ministry of National Defense replied, "Chinese laws prohibit any action including hacking that damages Internet security.... To accuse the Chinese military of launching cyber attacks without solid proof is unprofessional and baseless."

The Great Firewall of China

The Great Wall of China is a series of massive stone walls in the northern part of the country that once protected China from invaders. Named for this famous wall, the Great Firewall of China is an elaborate censorship system that prevents Chinese citizens from using the Internet to read or post material that the government finds objectionable. China is controlled by the Chinese Communist Party (CCP), and citizens are not free to criticize the party or its policies. Anyone who does so risks severe punishment.

To keep the Chinese Internet free of controversial material, the Chinese government blacklists certain IP addresses and automatically blocks connections to them. Most Internet traffic from outside China is blocked. Software constantly scans Internet traffic moving within China for banned keywords and terms, such as "human rights abuses." Searches for such terms often lead to dummy websites with pro-government messages.

The government also employs people to monitor Internet forums, social networking sites, and blogs for banned content and to delete it. People are also paid to make pro-CCP statements on online chats. Chinese businesses and organizations that violate censorship rules can be fined or shut down, so most organizations censor their own websites, making sure that questionable content never gets posted.

Some Chinese citizens have tried to evade the censors by using virtual private networks (VPNs). These networks encrypt data, hide information from keyword filters, and route traffic around government controls. But in 2012, the government installed new software to block VPN traffic in China. Explains Jon Penney of Harvard University, "The CCP is deeply committed to internet censorship and surveillance, in order to control information, stifle dissent, and shape public opinion."

China is not the only nation that uses the Internet to suppress dissent and to disseminate propaganda. Many countries practice some form of Internet censorship, with tactics similar to those used in China. Among the most repressive are Burma, Cuba, Saudi Arabia, Iran, Syria, Tunisia, Vietnam, and Turkmenistan.

US security experts don't buy it. Chinese attacks on US organizations have mostly followed a similar pattern. The hackers first infect computer systems at universities, small companies, and Internet service providers across the United States. They send their attacks via the infected US computers to disguise the true source of the hack. The hackers also continually switch from one IP address to another as they work, further confusing those who try to follow their trail.

"If you look at each attack in isolation, you can't say, 'This is the Chinese military,'" said Richard Bejtlich of the computer security company Mandiant. But he explained that on closer examination, patterns and similarities begin to emerge. "When you see the same group steal data on Chinese dissidents and Tibetan activists, then attack an aerospace company, it starts to push you in the right direction." Computer experts have also identified certain strains of malware that are used frequently in attacks originating from China.

Two Can Play This Game

As a result of mounting cyber attacks from China, the US government wanted to send a message to China that further hacking would not be tolerated. In May 2014, the US Justice Department charged five Chinese hackers—all of them PLA officers—with economic espionage and theft of trade secrets in the attack on Alcoa and the other Pennsylvania companies. China denied that its officers had any involvement in hacking and described the charges as absurd. In fact, the Chinese government charged that US government agencies were themselves tapping into China's government offices, corporations, and universities.

Revelations about NSA spying from the Snowden leaks show that this accusation is true. Leaked NSA documents detail extensive US spying on Chinese telephone networks, military units, and government offices. A major NSA target in China is

The Chinese company Huawei makes smartphones and other telecommunications equipment. Suspecting that Huawei is linked to the Chinese military, the NSA has hacked into the company's computer networks.

the telecommunications giant Huawei, which manufactures Internet software, routers, servers, and undersea cables, as well as smartphones and other networking technology. In an operation code-named Shotgiant, the NSA invaded Huawei's computers to look for links between the company and the PLA. The NSA also hoped to place surveillance equipment on phones, computers, and other products that Huawei sells in other nations, including Iran and Cuba. With such equipment, the United States could spy on these and other enemies. "Many of our targets [enemies] communicate over Huawei-produced products," a leaked 2010 NSA document revealed. "We want to make sure that we know how to exploit these products ... to gain access to networks of interest."

The US government acknowledges that it spies on foreign businesses and organizations. But it claims that it does so

> "Many of our targets [enemies] communicate over Huawei-produced products. We want to make sure that we know how to exploit these products ... to gain access to networks of interest."
>
> —National Security Agency document, discussing NSA spying on Chinese telecommunications company Huawei, 2010

not to steal business secrets but for national security purposes, since in many countries, businesses are actually agents of the government. For instance, the United States suspects that Huawei and many other businesses in China are arms of the Chinese military. As the leaked 2010 document about spying on Huawei explained, "If we can determine the company's plans and intentions, we hope that this will lead us back to the [military] plans and intentions of the PRC [People's Republic of China]."

Digital Cold War

Between 1945 and 1991, the United States and the former Soviet Union were engaged in the tense, often frightening Cold War. The two nations never engaged each other in direct military conflict (a hot war). However, they took opposing sides politically in various wars around the world, supplied weapons to each other's enemies, spied on each other, and viciously denounced each other through the media. The two nations also competed fiercely in weapons technology and space exploration.

Some twenty-first-century commentators remark that the United States and China are in a *digital* cold war. The cyber spying, denunciations, and mistrust marking the relationship between the two nations is reminiscent of the Soviet era. Yet at the same time, the United States trades extensively with China. In 2013 the United States exported more than $100 billion in goods to China and imported about $450 billion in goods from China. Both nations rely on this business for their economic health. Scholar Noah Feldman suggests that instead of fighting a cold war, the United States and China are engaged in a "cool war," marked by a "strange combination of competition and cooperation."

This cool war might someday turn hot, however. In their quest to gather data from US computers, Chinese hackers have not ignored the weapons of war. They have aggressively targeted computer systems of the Pentagon, the headquarters of the

Every day, cargo ships carry millions of dollars worth of goods between China and the United States. The two countries are important trading partners but also use cyber spying in an attempt to gain economic and military advantages over each other.

US Department of Defense, as well as other US military offices and defense manufacturers. The *Washington Post* reported that Chinese hackers have stolen designs and technical data involving the US Patriot missile system, US Army and Navy ballistic-missile defense systems, the F/A-18 fighter jet, the V-22 Osprey aircraft, the Black Hawk helicopter, the F-35 Joint Strike Fighter, and other weapons and weapons systems. The stolen data has enabled China to build similar equipment by copying US plans, without having to invest billions of dollars in research and development. US military officials worry that in the event of a war with China, the stolen plans would put the United States at a disadvantage. They fear that the Chinese would be able to use their technical knowledge of US weapons systems to remotely jam, crash, or otherwise disable them.

41

Chapter 5

Strong-Arm Tactics

IN THE TWENTIETH CENTURY, ARMIES FOUGHT ONE ANOTHER WITH GUNS, TANKS, AND BOMBS. In the twenty-first century, a new tool—the cyber attack—has entered the arena. During armed conflicts, modern nations still use bombs, missiles, and other weapons to damage enemy equipment, troops, and physical structures. But armies might also use cyber attacks to cripple enemy communications systems, financial systems, and computer-controlled infrastructure.

Whereas tanks and bombs cost millions of dollars to build, cyber attacks can be carried out very cheaply. "[A cyber attack] costs about four cents per machine," Internet researcher Bill Woodcock says. "You could fund an entire cyber warfare campaign for the cost of replacing a tank tread, so you would be foolish not to."

Cyber attacks are not likely to replace the physical weapons of war. However, "any modern conflict will include a cyber warfare component simply because it's too inexpensive to pass up," explains Woodcock.

E-war

Russia has used the Internet to fight its foes on several occasions. For example, in April 2007, the small northern European nation of Estonia, which had gained independence from the Russian-controlled Soviet Union in 1991, angered its Russian neighbor. In the Estonian capital of Tallinn, government officials relocated a memorial to Russian military men who had been killed in World War II (1939–1945). They moved it from a prominent spot in the town square to a military cemetery on the edge of the city.

Estonians saw the memorial as a bitter reminder of the Soviet occupation of their country. Russians saw its removal as an insult to Russian soldiers who had died in the war. The removal of the shrine triggered riots among Russians living in Estonia. One person was killed and 150 were injured in the melee.

Soon afterward, Estonia came under cyber attack. For three weeks, hackers hit Estonian government websites at the highest levels, including those of the parliament and various ministries. DDoS attacks shut down banks and media outlets. An estimated one million zombie computers took part in the attacks— bombarding Estonian computer systems with one thousand times their normal level of traffic.

Estonia has earned the nickname E-stonia for its high level of Internet connectivity. "Estonia depends largely on the Internet," explained Mikhail Tammet, head of Internet security in the nation's defense ministry. "We have e-government, government is so-called paperless . . . all the bank services are on the Internet. We even elect our parliament via the Internet."

The attack on Estonia's computers could have been catastrophic in such an Internet-dependent nation. But Estonia also has a sophisticated system of cyber security, and it was able to fight back. In a first step, Estonia's Computer Emergency Response Team (CERT) bolstered the nation's server capacity, to better handle all the incoming traffic. Then, working with the world's largest Internet service providers, Estonia identified hundreds of thousands of attacking zombie computers and knocked them off-line. The results of the attack were modest. The Estonian parliament's e-mail system was inoperable for four days, customers of the nation's two largest banks couldn't access their accounts for a few hours, and Estonian news outlets were temporarily disabled.

Estonian prime minister Andrus Ansip believed the massive attacks were perpetrated by Russia in retaliation for the removal of the statue. International investigators found that many of the attacking computers were indeed linked with Russian government offices. But Russian leaders denied any involvement in the attacks and refused to cooperate in the search for culprits. When a number of Russian citizens were identified as suspects, Russian officials refused to help prosecute them. In 2009 a pro-Russian government youth group called Nashi claimed responsibility for the attacks, but Russia took no action to punish Nashi.

> **"You could fund an entire cyber warfare campaign for the cost of replacing a tank tread, so you would be foolish not to."**
>
> — Bill Woodcock, *Internet researcher, 2008*

StopGeorgia.ru

When tensions flared between Russia and neighboring Georgia (also a former state of the Soviet Union) in July 2008, the Russians again resorted to cyber warfare. The disagreement involved a tiny area called South Ossetia, which was under Georgian control. Many South Ossetians wanted independence from Georgia, a change that the Russian government supported.

Russia did not intervene militarily at first. Instead, it launched a cyber war. While its troops mobilized along the South Ossetian border, hackers working with Russia's government launched Internet attacks on Georgian computers. On a website called StopGeorgia.ru, hackers could find a list of Georgian websites to attack and instructions on how to launch various strikes, such as DDoS attacks.

Among the hackers' targets was the website of Georgian president Mikheil Saakashvili, as well as sites of the nation's parliament, foreign ministry, news agencies, and banks. To express their disdain for Georgia, hackers placed images of

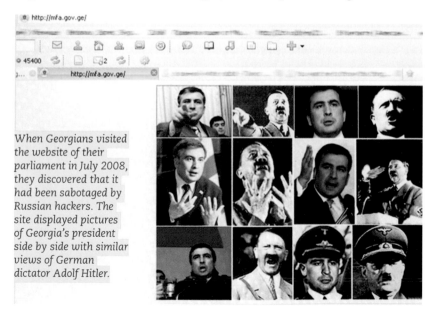

When Georgians visited the website of their parliament in July 2008, they discovered that it had been sabotaged by Russian hackers. The site displayed pictures of Georgia's president side by side with similar views of German dictator Adolf Hitler.

Saakashvili on the parliament's website next to photos of the much-despised Adolf Hitler, who had ruled Germany as a murderous dictator during World War II.

The attacks continued for several weeks and temporarily disrupted Georgian government and businesses. Then the Russians began a traditional war by sending troops into South Ossetia. The offensive lasted for four days and ended with a Russian victory.

After the war, the Russian government denied its involvement in the cyber attacks, but security researchers concluded that it had been responsible. The nonprofit US Cyber Consequences Unit, an independent research group, backed that analysis, reporting that a first wave of cyber strikes had been coordinated with Russian military operations. The unit confirmed that a second wave of cyber attacks had been launched by proponents of the Russian government.

No Nukes

Cyber warfare has also become a tool in nuclear showdowns. The United States and Russia both have large stockpiles of nuclear weapons—capable of destroying all life on Earth. The United Kingdom, France, China, India, Pakistan, North Korea, and Israel have smaller numbers of nuclear weapons. The United States is determined to prevent other nations, particularly enemies such as Iran, from developing nuclear bombs and has used cyber warfare to make sure that doesn't happen.

Creating nuclear weapons or nuclear power involves enriching uranium, or changing its chemical composition. This is done inside large spinning cylinders called centrifuges, which process the uranium isotopes U-235 and U-238 to create a mixture that is capable of producing energy.

In 2006 Iran revived a uranium enrichment program at an underground site called Natanz in central Iran. Iranian president Mahmoud Ahmadinejad claimed that the facility was being used

Iranian president Mahmoud Ahmadinejad (front) claimed that these centrifuges would be used to create nuclear energy for his nation. US leaders thought the centrifuges would be used instead to build nuclear bombs. By infecting computers that controlled the centrifuges with malware, the United States was able to destroy some of the machines.

to enrich uranium for nuclear power, a peaceful application. The United States was dubious and worried that the enriched uranium would be used to make nuclear bombs. US president George W. Bush wanted to shut down the operation but did not want to use military strikes in Iran, since the United States was already at war in nearby Iraq and did not want to inflame the region further. The plan instead was a cyber attack on the computers at Natanz to disable the five thousand centrifuges there.

The National Security Agency took charge of the operation, code-named Olympic Games. (It was supposed to be top secret, but officials who worked on the program later described the events to author and *New York Times* journalist David Sanger.) First, the NSA infected the Natanz computers with a code that electronically mapped operations at the facility and the

47

Flash Point

For protection against malware, the computers that control the centrifuges at Natanz are not connected to the Internet. So how did the NSA unleash Stuxnet into the computers there? According to insiders, an Iranian saboteur—employed at the plant but secretly working for the United States and Israel—snuck it into the plant on a flash drive.

workings of its centrifuges. With this information in hand, cyber specialists from the NSA and from Israel, a US ally, created a complex worm to attack the centrifuges. Dubbed "the bug" by its creators, the worm performed extremely well in tests. It could speed up or slow down a centrifuge so suddenly that its delicate mechanical parts broke apart.

The bug made its first attacks in 2008, successfully disabling some centrifuges at Natanz. When US president Barack Obama took office in 2009, he authorized further, more aggressive cyber attacks on the facility. Computer experts created a new version of the bug and sent it to Natanz, but in the summer of 2010, something went amiss. The bug was designed to work only within the facility at Natanz. An error in the code, however, allowed the bug to leave the facility via employee laptop computers and then to replicate itself across the Internet. When computer security experts found the worm, they renamed it Stuxnet—a combination of several keywords contained in the software.

With the worm exposed, President Obama pondered whether to shut down Olympic Games. In the end, he decided to continue with the attacks that summer, successfully destroying nearly one thousand centrifuges at Natanz and temporarily slowing down

Iran's nuclear weapons program. Following that attack, Iranian security experts figured out how to detect Stuxnet and remove it from computers.

Flamethrowers

Following Stuxnet, between 2010 and 2012, Iran was attacked by a sophisticated virus called Flame. Most computer experts believe that the United States and Israel were behind the Flame attacks, although neither nation has admitted to any involvement. Security experts note that Flame and Stuxnet contain some of the same code, so they were likely written by some of the same people. Tom Parker of the security firm FusionX remarked, "This is not something that most security researchers have the skills or resources to do. You'd expect [the virus to be from] only the most advanced [mathematicians], such as those working at NSA."

Flame is designed for cyber espionage. It can penetrate even the most secure networks to activate computer microphones and cameras, record keystrokes, take screen shots, and extract data. After gathering the data it wants, Flame can also wipe everything from a computer's hard drive, leaving the victim without critical files. The Flame attacks on Iran were directed at the nation's oil industry, which dominates Iran's economy. Once the virus was detected, Iran had to temporarily shut down its oil ministry, some of its oil rigs, and a major oil terminal to prevent the spread of the virus.

To retaliate, Iranian hackers, calling themselves the Cutting Sword of Justice, unleashed a virus in August 2012 against the Saudi Arabian Oil Company (Saudi Aramco), which has close ties to US oil companies. The virus erased documents, spreadsheets, e-mails, and other important files on about thirty thousand oil company computers. In place of the destroyed data, the attackers posted an image of a burning American flag. A few weeks later, Iranian hackers hit RasGas, a natural gas company in the Middle Eastern nation of Qatar, also with close ties to the United States. The hackers were able to temporarily shut down the RasGas website. Next came DDoS attacks against top US banks, including JPMorgan Chase, Wells Fargo, and Capital One. US investigators have linked the attacks to fewer than one hundred Iranian computer specialists with ties to the Iranian government.

The Iranian attacks, especially against Aramco, were effective in disrupting business operations. The attacks "proved you don't have to be sophisticated to do a lot of damage," said Richard A. Clarke, a former counterterrorism official at the US National Security Council. "There are lots of targets in the U.S. where they could do the same thing. The attacks were intended to say: 'If you mess with us, you can expect retaliation.'"

On the Campaign Trail

Cyber attacks can also be used for political destabilization. Politicians commonly use the Internet in campaigns. They rally their supporters using websites, Twitter feeds, and other online social media. But unscrupulous opponents can attack or hijack these same online efforts fairly easily. For instance, during the 2012 presidential elections in Mexico, the Institutional Revolutionary Party (known by the initials of its Spanish name, PRI) reportedly used tens of thousands of bots to post misleading messages on opposing parties' Twitter feeds and Facebook pages. The messages confused voters, and the PRI candidate won the election.

In Syria, a group called the Syrian Electronic Army, supporters of dictatorial president Bashar al-Assad, has attacked the computers of Assad's political enemies using Blackshades and other malware. It has also hacked into the Twitter feeds of Al Jazeera, the Associated Press, the British Broadcasting Corporation, Reuters, and other global news organizations to post pro-Assad tweets.

Hack the Vote

In March 2013, the United States had its first case of election cyber fraud when an election website in Miami-Dade County, Florida, received twenty-five hundred fraudulent requests for absentee ballots. The requests came from a small number of IP addresses in Ireland, the United Kingdom, India, and other foreign nations. Election workers immediately recognized the requests as fraudulent and blocked further communication from the IP addresses. The election, which involved races for local, state, and congressional offices, proceeded as normal, without any further concerns about fraud.

But computer security experts worry that future elections could be hijacked or disrupted by hackers by one of the following means:

- *Malware used to change votes inside digital voting machines*
- *Malware inserted on personal computers to change votes in an online election*
- *DDoS attacks on election servers*
- *"Spoof" election websites that look like the real thing, leading voters to believe they have cast valid ballots when they haven't*

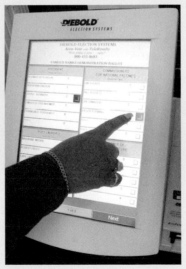

In 2012 a worker at a US Department of Energy laboratory set out to see how hard it would be to hack into a touch-screen digital voting machine—the type used in twenty US states. Using thirty dollars' worth of electronics gear he bought from RadioShack, the worker was able to hack into a machine and program it to change votes. Once he had the technique figured out, it took less than a minute to execute the hack.

In the United States, many people cast ballots using digital voting machines. Security experts fear that hackers could tamper with machines to change the outcome of elections.

Around the world, police, government agencies, and other organizations frequently hack into the websites of political activists. For example, hackers have repeatedly hit websites affiliated with the fourteenth Dalai Lama, the spiritual leader of the Tibetan people, in retaliation for his public stance against Chinese human rights abuses. In 2013 hackers defaced oct26driving.org, a website that rallied women in Saudi Arabia (who are by law subservient to men) to protest the nation's ban on female drivers. The site organized women to take the wheel on October 26, and the action went forward as planned, despite the hacking.

The hacktivist group Anonymous often posts pictures and messages on the websites of its targets. A masked character—based on the image of seventeenth-century British rebel Guy Fawkes—is the group's logo.

Other times, activists are the ones doing the hacking. Anonymous—a loose association of US, UK, and other hackers— is the world's most famous group of hacktivists. Since the first decade of the 2000s, it has attacked the computer systems of dozens of people and organizations, many of them with conservative social agendas. The group's targets include the Church of Scientology, Sarah Palin (the Republican US vice presidential candidate in 2008), the US Tea Party movement, the Vatican (the headquarters of the Roman Catholic Church), and the antigay Westboro Baptist Church. The group's most common assault method is the DDoS. Anonymous has also defaced websites and stolen private data from sites.

Chapter 6

Dee-Fense!

WE'VE ALL HEARD THE WARNINGS ABOUT PROTECTING OURSELVES FROM CYBER CRIME: install security software on your computer and keep it up to date; don't open attachments from anyone you don't know; and create strong passwords (with a combination of numerals, symbols, and lowercase and uppercase letters), change them often, and never use the same password for more than one account. That's all good advice, but it won't guarantee that you won't get hacked.

For one thing, security software isn't foolproof. The *New York Times* discovered that in 2013 after it was hit by Chinese cyber criminals. The *Times* thought its computers were protected by Symantec security software. But when hackers installed forty-five pieces of malware on the newspaper's computers, the security software discovered only one of them.

As for not opening suspicious attachments, it's easy to see how people can get tricked into doing just that. Using lists of

Facebook friends and other contacts, cyber criminals can craft e-mails that look as if they come from a friend, a coworker, or a family member. But even careful avoidance of anything suspicious that arrives via e-mail isn't sufficient. All it takes is one visit to an infected website to infect your computer. For example, in 2012 hackers installed malware on the website GoDaddy.com. When people visited GoDaddy (which provides web services), the malware passed ransomware to their computers.

As for passwords, they aren't that hard to crack. In fact, password cracking software is widely available online. The programs run through billions of combinations of letters, numbers, and symbols until they hit on the password they're looking for. A password consisting of six lowercase letters can be found out by a cracking program in just ten minutes.

The Good Guys

Hacking into computers is against the law, and when they are discovered, hackers are arrested, charged, and punished. Depending on the nature of the crime, punishment can range from community service to fines to long prison sentences. In the United States, various local, state, and federal government agencies have specialized cyber crime units. At the federal level, the FBI, the Secret Service, Immigration and Customs Enforcement, the Department of Homeland Security, and other agencies all pursue cyber criminals. Foreign countries have their own agencies for fighting cyber crime.

But for every bad guy the authorities lock up, tens of thousands remain free. That's because tracking down cyber criminals is much harder than looking for more traditional criminals. Hackers are experts at disguising their identities behind botnets, hijacked servers, and online aliases. And even when law enforcement does catch a hacker, prosecuting the crime can be difficult—especially if the criminal is a citizen of a foreign nation. For instance, even though the United States charged five Chinese military officers

Mobile Devices: The Weakest Link

More and more, people are bypassing personal computers in favor of smartphones, tablets, and other mobile devices. Many people use mobile devices for financial transactions, such as online banking. A new trend is the use of mobile wallets, which enable purchases using credit card numbers stored on a smartphone.

Of course, cyber criminals know about the trends and have created malware specifically to infect mobile devices. Mobile malware can record data typed into a device, such as bank account numbers, PINs, and credit card numbers. It can search through text messages, e-mails, and other files to find sensitive information. Cyber criminals use infected apps and phishing texts to infect mobile devices with malware. In the summer of 2014, smartphone users began to report ransomware attacks, with about 900,000 phones affected in just one month.

Experts say that mobile devices may be even more vulnerable to cyber crime than personal computers because people more often use them on insecure Wi-Fi connections. What's more, people who use personal mobile devices at work might unwittingly contaminate their business networks by using an infected device on the job.

Most mobile devices come with built-in security features, such as password protection or PINs. But a 2013 survey by trade group CTIA (formerly called the Cellular Telecommunications Industry Association) revealed that fewer than half of all mobile device owners use these features.

For further protection, some people download security software designed specifically for their mobile devices. But another survey, this one conducted by Symantec, showed that worldwide, only 17 percent of smartphone users had installed such software on their phones. More than half of those surveyed didn't even know that mobile security software was available.

More than two-thirds of Americans have smartphones, and hackers have designed malware specifically to target these devices. Security software is available, but most smartphone users don't have it.

The US DoJ worked with law enforcement agencies from eighteen other nations to shut down a worldwide Blackshades distribution network. In May 2014, a DOJ attorney spoke at a press conference about the operation, which resulted in more than ninety arrests.

with cyber crimes in 2014, the chances of them being imprisoned for their crimes are slim to none. China denies that its officers were involved in any hacking and will not cooperate to release them to the United States to be tried and punished.

On the other hand, many nations do work together to fight cyber crime. More than fifty countries, including the United States, have signed on to the Budapest Convention on Cybercrime, which went into effect in 2004. The convention sets official definitions for different types of cyber crimes, provides guidelines for investigating and prosecuting the crimes, and outlines ways for nations to cooperate in the pursuit of cyber criminals. International associations such as the United Nations, the International Telecommunication Union, the Group of Eight (an association of leading industrialized nations), and the European Union also have anti–cyber crime units, enabling nations to coordinate efforts in the fight against cyber crime.

When it comes to cyber warfare, however, international protocols are not yet in place. In the 1800s and the 1900s, nations around the world signed on to a series of treaties called the Geneva Conventions. The conventions outline rules to be followed by warring nations and call for the humane treatment of wounded soldiers, prisoners of war, and civilians. Some modern commentators have called for new conventions to create rules for cyber warfare. Such rules might prohibit attacks on hospital computers, for example, to guarantee that people who are sick or wounded can continue to receive the care they need, even during wartime.

Many experts believe that the best cyber defense is a good cyber offense. They advocate striking cyber attackers before they have a chance to attack. In many cases, potential targets note suspicious or increased activity on their websites, clues that a cyber attack might be coming. In fall 2012, President Barack Obama signed a directive that would allow an offensive cyber attack if the United States learned of an imminent or ongoing cyber threat from an enemy. "Suppose that somebody's sending a signal to freeze all our computer networks," explained an Obama administration official. "I think most people would agree that we can neutralize that virus and we can do that in self-defense. You don't have to wait until they paralyze the server, because, once they do, the damage is done."

Fighting Fire with Fire

For businesses, fending off cyber attacks can be frustrating. "We are not winning the cyber war," wrote security expert Brian Finch on the Fox News website in June 2014. He noted that 97 percent of US businesses had suffered some form of cyber intrusion and that the "mountain of money" being spent on cyber defense was barely making a dent in the number of successful cyber attacks. Cyber security expert Michael Walker explains, "The cost for defenders trying to block every possible weakness is so much greater than the cost of attackers, to be able to find one way in."

What can be done to improve defenses? Some companies are trying to beat the hackers at their own game. Tactics include planting false blueprints and other information on servers, so that thieves who make a successful attack end up with something worthless. Intelligence expert Jeffery L. Stutzman suggests tagging top-secret documents so that if they're stolen, they will self-destruct or send a signal back to the rightful owners.

In 2013 the Defense Advanced Research Projects Agency (DARPA, the US Department of Defense group that created the forerunner of the Internet in the 1960s) decided to put the world's best computer minds to work on the problem. It announced a contest called the Cyber Grand Challenge, with cash prizes going to teams that develop fully automated, self-defending computer systems. The winning system will be able to detect intruders, identify the coding errors that allow them to enter a network, and automatically make the necessary repairs. The program would have no need for human involvement and would operate with no disruption to ordinary computing tasks, such as receiving and sending e-mails. By June 2014, thirty-five teams had entered the contest. They will have two years to complete their projects.

DARPA's Daniel Kaufman admitted that perfect computer security is unattainable. But with a self-defending system, Internet security could be greatly strengthened. "It's not like the bad guys are going to say, 'Well played, DARPA—we give up,'" Kaufman said. "But if nothing else, we will have eliminated easy attacks and raised the cost to them of any attack."

> "The cost for defenders trying to block every possible weakness [in a computer system] is so much greater than the cost of attackers, to be able to find one way in."
>
> — Michael Walker, cyber security expert, 2014

Dee-Fense!

Future Shock

The future of cyber warfare remains unclear. Some people worry about viruses shutting down power grids, sending entire cities into darkness. Others talk about coordinated attacks on banks and other financial institutions that will wreak havoc with world economies. In 2012 former US defense secretary Leon Panetta warned about hackers sending passenger trains

Power Grab

In 2012 researchers began noticing aggressive and sophisticated cyber attacks on North American and European oil and gas companies, energy grid operators, electrical generation firms, and petroleum pipeline operators. The hackers work from 9 a.m. to 6 p.m., Monday through Friday, Moscow time, leading to the belief that they are Russian and also leading to the operation's nickname, Energetic Bear. (The bear is a symbol of Russia.)

The sophistication and strength of the attacks suggest that the hackers have the backing of the Russian government. Some experts

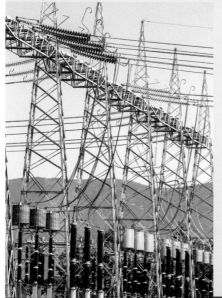

think they are engaged in industrial espionage—looking for business secrets to pass on to Russian energy firms. Others worry that the attacks could lead to sabotage—the deliberate destruction of energy infrastructures in the United States and elsewhere.

In the United States and elsewhere, electric power grids, oil and gas pipelines, transportation systems, and water systems are all controlled by computers. Security experts say that in the event of war, an enemy might target such infrastructures with malware, potentially leaving citizens without water, power, or means of long-distance travel.

careening off railroad tracks and poisoning water supplies. But many dismiss such scenarios as far-fetched. They argue that such attacks, especially on a large nation like the United States, would do only limited and short-term damage.

The damage would be much more severe if a nation's nuclear stockpiles were attacked. Thomas D'Agostino, former head of the US National Nuclear Security Administration, explained that US nuclear labs "are under constant attack" from hackers looking to steal nuclear-technology secrets. To prevent enemies from taking remote control of US nuclear weapons, the systems that control these weapons are "airgapped"—that is, they are disconnected from the Internet. But "airgapping is not a perfect defense," explains Adam Segal, a cyber security expert with the Council on Foreign Relations. "Even in secure systems, people stick in their thumb drives, they go back and forth between computers.... If [hackers] put enough attention to it, they can possibly be penetrated."

Specialists at the US Navy Cyber Defense Operations Command monitor navy computer systems around the clock, looking for unauthorized activity on the network.

Dee-Fense!

To prepare for whatever the future may hold, the United States has beefed up its cyber defense abilities. In 2013 the Pentagon announced that it would nearly quintuple its cyber security staff, going from nine hundred employees to just under five thousand in two years. The increased staff will not only allow the United States to better defend itself against cyber espionage, but it will also allow the nation to carry out more aggressive attacks on enemy nations.

Some commentators have criticized the increase. They say that US leaders have exaggerated the threat of cyber attacks to stir up fear among the American people, beef up US military dominance around the world, and direct more taxpayer dollars to the Pentagon and military contractors. They also worry that increased government cyber security will further strengthen the surveillance power of the NSA and further weaken online privacy and freedom for US citizens.

Anything Goes

Many people have compared cyber space to the Wild West, an era on the US western frontier when bandits and gunmen roamed far and wide, law-enforcement officers were few and far between, and people took the law into their own hands. Chances are cyber space will remain similarly lawless for many years to come. In the shadowy online world, it's not hard for cyber criminals to stay one step ahead of the law. Brian Finch explains, "It is only a matter of months, if not less, before cyber attackers can create new techniques to evade newly created defenses." He notes that attackers often use a piece of malicious code just one time and then switch to something new. Defenders don't know what to look out for next, and old defenses become useless.

How can you completely protect yourself from cyber attacks? You could cancel your Internet service, ditch your cell phone, close your bank account, throw away your debit card, and turn off your electricity. You could quit school and never take a job, vote in an election, get a driver's license, or fly on an airplane. Of course, such a solution is completely unrealistic. We live in a wired world, with all its benefits and risks. As Italian philosopher and writer Umberto Eco stresses, "The Web is not something we can discard; like the power loom, automobile and television before it, the Web is here to stay. Nothing, not even dictatorships, will ever eliminate it. So the question is not how to recognize the Internet's inherent risks, but how to make the best use of it."

And as for cyber warfare, Eugene Kaspersky, founder and CEO of the Internet security firm Kaspersky Lab, sums up, "It's not a question of if a major cyber warfare attack will happen—it's an issue of when and how bad it will be.... We have to think and accept that as a reality. We live in a dangerous world."

Source Notes

9   Phil Lapsley, "The Definitive Story of Steve Wozniak, Steve Jobs, and Phone Phreaking," *Atlantic,* February 20, 2013, http://www.theatlantic.com /technology/archive/2013/02/the-definitive-story-of-steve-wozniak-steve -jobs-and-phone-phreaking/273331/.

11 Sharon Gaudin, "Computer Sabotage Verdict Set Aside," *Computerworld,* July 17, 2000, http://www.computerworld.com/s/article/47212/Computer _sabotage_verdict_set_aside.

18 Lauren Schutte, "Miss Teen USA Reveals Cyberstalking and Extortion Plot," *Yahoo! Celebrity,* August 13, 2013, http://celebrity.yahoo.com/blogs/celeb-news /miss-teen-usa-reveals-cyberstalking-extortion-plot-201005569.html.

21 Griff White, "Snowden Says Government Spying Worse than Orwellian," *WashingtonPost.com,* December 25, 2013, http://www.washingtonpost.com /world/europe/snowden-says-spying-worse-than-orwellian/2013/12/25 /e9c806aa-6d90-11e3-a5d0-6f31cd74f760_story.html.

22 Gerry Smith, "'Snowden Effect.' Threatens US Tech Industry's Global Ambitions," *HuffingtonPost.com,* January 24, 2014, http://www.huffingtonpost .com/2014/01/24/edward-snowden-tech-industry_n_4596162.html.

24 "Willie Sutton," Federal Bureau of Investigation, accessed August 2, 2014, http://www.fbi.gov/about-us/history/famous-cases/willie-sutton.

28 Elizabeth A. Harris, Nicole Perlroth, Nathaniel Popper, and Hilary Stout, "A Sneaky Path into Target Customers' Wallets," *New York Times,* January 17, 2014, http://www.nytimes.com/2014/01/18/business/a-sneaky-path-into -target-customers-wallets.html?module=Search&mabReward=relbias%3Ar% 2C[%22RI%3A6%22%2C%22RI%3A17%22].

32 Parmy Olson, *We Are Anonymous: Inside the Hacker World of LulzSec, Anonymous, and the Global Cyber Insurgency* (New York: Little, Brown, 2012), 114.

32 Ibid., 114–115.

36 Nicole Perlroth, "Hackers in China Attacked the *Times* for Last 4 Months," *New York Times,* January 30, 2013, http://www.nytimes.com/2013/01/31 /technology/chinese-hackers-infiltrate-new-york-times-computers .html?pagewanted=al.

37 "The Great Firewall of China," *openDemocracy,* March 15, 2013, http://www .opendemocracy.net/china-correspondent/great-firewall-of-china.

38 Perlroth, "Hackers in China."

39 David E. Sanger and Nicole Perlroth, "N.S.A. Breached Chinese Servers Seen as Security Threat," *New York Times,* March 22, 2014, http://www.nytimes .com/2014/03/23/world/asia/nsa-breached-chinese-servers-seen-as-spy -peril.html.

40 Ibid.

41 Elise Hu, "The 'Cool War' with China Is Unseen, but Comes with Consequences," *National Public Radio,* June 6, 2014, http://www.npr.org/blogs/parallels/2014/06/06/318788569/the-cool-war-with-china-is-unseen-but-comes-with-consequences.

43 John Markoff, "Before the Gunfire, Cyberattacks," *New York Times,* August 12, 2008, http://www.nytimes.com/2008/08/13/technology/13cyber.html?_r=0.

43 Ben Arnoldy, "Cyberspace: New Frontier in Conflicts," *Christian Science Monitor,* August 13, 2008, http://www.csmonitor.com/USA/Military/2008/0813/p01s05-usmi.html.

43 "Estonia Hit by 'Moscow Cyber War,'" *BBC News,* May 17, 2007, http://news.bbc.co.uk/2/hi/europe/6665145.stm.

49 Ellen Nakashima, Greg Miller, and Julie Tate, "U.S., Israel Developed Flame Computer Virus to Slow Iranian Nuclear Efforts, Officials Say," *Washington Post,* June 19, 2012, http://www.washingtonpost.com/world/national-security/us-israel-developed-computer-virus-to-slow-iranian-nuclear-efforts-officials-say/2012/06/19/gJQA6xBPoV_story.html.

50 Nicole Perlroth, "In Cyberattack on Saudi Firm, U.S. Sees Iran Fighting Back," *New York Times,* October 23, 2012, http://www.nytimes.com/2012/10/24/business/global/cyberattack-on-saudi-oil-firm-disquiets-us.html?pagewanted=all.

58 Ellen Nakashima, "In Cyberwarfare, Rules of Engagement Still Hard to Define," *Washington Post,* March 10, 2013, http://www.washingtonpost.com/world/national-security/in-cyberwarfare-rules-of-engagement-still-hard-to-define/2013/03/10/0442507c-88da-11e2-9d71-f0feafdd1394_story.html.

58 Brian Finch, "Rethinking Cyber Defense," *Fox Business,* June 24, 2014, http://www.foxbusiness.com/technology/2014/06/24/rethinking-cyber-defense/.

58 Kenneth Change, "Automating Cybersecurity," *New York Times,* June 2, 2014, http://www.nytimes.com/2014/06/03/science/automating-cybersecurity.html.

60 Ibid.

61 Jason Koebler, "U.S. Nukes Face up to 10 Million Cyber Attacks Daily," *U.S. News and World Report,* March 20, 2012, http://www.usnews.com/news/articles/2012/03/20/us-nukes-face-up-to-10-million-cyber-attacks-daily.

62 Ibid.

62 Finch, "Rethinking Cyber Defense."

63 Umberto Eco, "The Web Is Here to Stay," *International Herald Tribune,* March 22, 2014, http://www.iht.com/2014/03/22/the-web-is-here-to-stay/.

63 Samantha Murphy Kelly, "Experts Say Looming Cyber Warfare Attacks Could Be 'Catastrophic,'" *Mashable,* January 30, 2013, http://mashable.com/2013/01/30/cyber-warfare/.

Selected Bibliography

Alterman, Elizabeth. "As Kids Go Online, Identity Theft Claims More Victims." *CNBC.com*, October 10, 2011. http://www.cnbc.com/id/44583556.

Angwin, Julia. *Dragnet Nation: A Quest for Privacy, Security, and Freedom in a World of Relentless Surveillance*. New York: Henry Holt, 2014.

Baldor, Lolita C. "Pentagon Takes Aim at China Cyber Threat." *Boston.com*, August 19, 2010. http://www.boston.com/news/nation/washington /articles/2010/08/19/pentagon_takes_aim_at_china_cyber_threat/?page=1.

Brenner, Joel. *American the Vulnerable: Inside the New Threat Matrix of Digital Espionage, Crime, and Warfare*. New York: Penguin Press, 2011.

Carr, Jeffrey. *Inside Cyber Warfare*. Sebastopol, CA: O'Reilly Media, 2010.

Clarke, Richard A. *Cyber War: The Next Threat to National Security and What to Do about It*. New York: HarperCollins, 2010.

"Estonia Hit by 'Moscow Cyber War.'" *BBC News*, May 17 , 2007. http://news .bbc.co.uk/2/hi/europe/6665145.stm.

Geers, Kenneth. "Cyberspace and the Changing Nature of Warfare." *SC Magazine*, August 27, 2008. http://www.scmagazine.com/cyberspace-and -the-changing-nature-of-warfare/article/115929/.

Glenny, Misha. *DarkMarket: Cyberthieves, Cybercops and You*. New York: Alfred A. Knopf, 2011.

Gorman, Siobhan, and Julian E. Barnes. "Iran Blamed for Cyberattacks." *Wall Street Journal*, October 12, 2012. http://online.wsj.com/news/articles/SB1000 08723963904446578045780529.1555576700.

James, Randy. "A Brief History of Cybercrime." *Time*, June 1, 2009. http:// content.time.com/time/nation/article/0,8599,1902073,00.html.

Kelly, Samantha Murphy. "Experts Say Looming Cyber Warfare Attacks Could Be 'Catastrophic.'" *Mashable*, January 30, 2013. http://mashable .com/2013/01/30/cyber-warfare/.

Lapsley, Phil. "The Definitive Story of Steve Wozniak, Steve Jobs, and Phone Phreaking." *Atlantic*, February 20, 2013. http://www.theatlantic.com /technology/archive/2013/02/the-definitive-story-of-steve-wozniak-steve -jobs-and-phone-phreaking/273331/.

Markoff, John. "Before the Gunfire, Cyberattacks." *New York Times*, August 12, 2008. http://www.nytimes.com/2008/08/13/technology/13cyber.html?_r=0.

Morganteen, Jeff. "How the Cybercrime Community Fueled Target Breach: McAfee." *CNBC.com*, March 10, 2014. http://www.cnbc.com/id/101480102.

Nakashima, Ellen. "In Cyberwarfare, Rules of Engagement Still Hard to Define." *Washington Post*, March 10, 2013. http://www.washingtonpost.com /world/national-security/in-cyberwarfare-rules-of-engagement-still-hard -to-define/2013/03/10/0442507c-88da-11e2-9d71-f0feafdd1394_story.html.

Olson, Parmy. *We Are Anonymous: Inside the Hacker World of LulzSec, Anonymous, and the Global Cyber Insurgency.* New York: Little, Brown, 2012.

Sanger, David E. "Obama Ordered Sped Up Waves of Cyberattacks against Iran." *New York Times,* June 1, 2012. http://www.nytimes.com/2012/06/01 /world/middleeast/obama-ordered-wave-of-cyberattacks-against-iran .html?pagewanted=all&_r=0.

Schutte, Lauren. "Miss Teen USA Reveals Cyberstalking and Extortion Plot." *Yahoo! Celebrity,* August 13, 2013. http://celebrity.yahoo.com/blogs/celeb -news/miss-teen-usa-reveals-cyberstalking-extortion-plot-201005569.html.

Shahid, Aliyah. "Pentagon Hacked, 24,000 Files Stolen by 'Foreign Intruders' in Cyber Attack." *New York Daily News,* July 14, 2011. http://www .nydailynews.com/news/national/pentagon-hacked-24-000-files-stolen -foreign-intruders-cyber-attack-article-1.156334.

Shekaraubi, Shahrooz. "The Wild West of Cyberwarfare." *International Policy Digest,* February 26, 2014. http://www.internationalpolicydigest. org/2014/02/26/the-wild-west-of-cyberwarfare/.

Weigant, Chris. "We Need a Geneva Convention on Cyber Warfare." *Huffington Post,* October 28, 2013. http://www.huffingtonpost.com/chris -weigant/we-need-a-geneva-conventi_b_4171853.html.

For Further Information

BOOKS

Doeden, Matt. *Steve Jobs: Technology Innovator and Apple Genius.* Minneapolis: Lerner Publications, 2012.

———. *Whistle-Blowers: Exposing Crime and Corruption.* Minneapolis: Twenty-First Century Books, 2015.

Espejo, Roman. *Policing the Internet.* Farmington Hills, MI: Greenhaven Press, 2012.

Falkner, Brian. *Brain Jack.* New York: Ember, 2011.

Greenwald, Glenn. *No Place to Hide: Edward Snowden, the NSA, and the U.S. Surveillance State.* New York: Metropolitan Books, 2014.

Mitnick, Kevin and William L. Song. *Ghost in the Wires: My Adventures as the World's Most Wanted Hacker.* New York: Little, Brown, 2011.

Mitra, Anandra. *Digital Security: Cyber Terror and Cyber Security.* New York: Chelsea House, 2010.

Singer, P. W., and Allan Friedman. *Cybersecurity and Cyberwar: What Everyone Needs to Know.* New York: Oxford University Press, 2014.

Zetter, Kim. *Countdown to Zero Day: Stuxnet and the Launch of the World's First Digital Weapon.* New York: Crown, 2014.

WEBSITES

Code Wars: America's Cyber Threat
http://www.cnbc.com/id/42210831#
A companion website to the 2011 CNBC TV special of the same name, this site offers videos about hacking, cyber war, and cyber security.

Computer History Museum
http://www.computerhistory.org/
Based in Mountain View, California, the Computer History Museum offers both brick-and-mortar and online exhibits about Internet history, microprocessors, computer pioneers, and more.

Cyber Crime
http://www.fbi.gov/about-us/investigate/cyber
The Federal Bureau of Investigation is on the front lines in fighting cyber crime in the United States. This FBI website includes a list of "Cyber's Most Wanted," details recent cyber crime cases and takedowns, and discusses methods for protecting against cyber crime.

Cybersecurity
http://www.dhs.gov/topic/cybersecurity
This website, created by the US Department of Homeland Security, offers advice on how to protect yourself against cyber crime and explains its own efforts to fight cyber crime.

FILM

We Are Legion: The Story of the Hacktivists. DVD. New York: FilmBuff, 2012.
This documentary film tells the story of the hacker collective Anonymous, which has grabbed headlines with its high-profile cyber attacks on political, religious, and financial organizations.

Index

Photo Acknowledgments

The images in this book are used with the permission of: NASA Earth Observatory/NOAA NGDC (Earth's city lights background); Courtesy of the FBI, p. 5; Courtesy of the Computer History Museum, p. 7; AP Photo/Steve Boitano, p. 12; © TommL/Getty Images, p. 16; © Paul A. Hebert/Press Line Photos/CORBIS, p. 18; © The Guardian via Getty Images, p. 20; Courtesy of United States Attorney's Office for the Southern District of New York, p. 25; © Joe Raedle/Getty Images, p. 27; © DNY59/Getty Images, p. 31; AP Photo/ Rex Features, p. 35; © Bloomberg/Getty Images, p. 39; © Stephen Finn/ Alamy, p. 41; Courtesy of Georgian Government Website, p. 45; AP Photo/ Photographer, p. 47; Jim Ruymen/Reuters/Newscom, p. 51; © ZUMA Press, Inc./Alamy, p. 52; © vita khorzhevska/Shutterstock.com, p. 56; © Andrew Burton/Getty Images, p. 57; © Antonio Ciufo/Getty Images, p. 60; US Navy photos provided by Navy Visual News Service, Washington, DC, p. 61.

Front cover: NASA Earth Observatory/NOAA NGDC.

About the Authors

Martin Gitlin has worked for two decades as a sportswriter and is also a freelance book writer and journalist based in Cleveland, Ohio. He has written history books for young adult readers, including works on the landmark *Brown v. Board of Education* case, the Battle of the Little Bighorn, and the stock market crash of 1929. He has also written biographies of NASCAR drivers Jimmie Johnson and Jeff Gordon.

Margaret J. Goldstein was born in Detroit and graduated from the University of Michigan. She has written and edited many books for young readers. She lives in northern New Mexico.